Keys:- Major: G C F
D   Bb
A

Minor: Am, Dm,

GRAPPELLI

THE VOCABULARY OF GYPSY JAZZ VIOLIN

by TIM KLIPHUIS

audio contents:

Online Audio   www.melbay.com/LP001MEB

INDEX

INTRODUCTION

Here it is. A serious look at the notes and melodies of the great French jazz maestro, Stéphane Grappelli!

My previous book **"Stéphane Grappelli - Gypsy Jazz Violin"** (purchase details on *www.stephanegrappelli.com*), gives an introduction to the Gypsy Jazz violin style. Its topics, such as timing, sound, accents, and how to play over chord changes, cover all the aspects in a general way, and the analysis of six classic Grappelli solos shows how it works in real time.

The book you are holding now takes things a bit further and looks at the *idiom* used by Grappelli, in other words his *notes*. If you want to sound more like a gypsy jazz violinist, this is the book for you. It teaches you lots of timeless Grappelli phrases that you can throw in during your solos, from different periods in his career.

I hope you have as much fun working with this book as I had writing it. If you have any questions, or if you want to find out about my other book, DVDs and videos, or the annual Grappelli workshop camp, here is where to go:

www.stephanegrappelli.com
www.timkliphuis.com

Or you can always send me an email at **info@timkliphuis.com**. One bit of advice: get your own band going and visit gypsy jam sessions whenever you can - it's the only way to practise your licks and solos.

Enjoy!

Tim Kliphuis, The Netherlands, 2012

ABOUT THE AUTHOR

Tim Kliphuis is widely recognised as the heir to Stéphane Grappelli's throne. As a performer, he has toured and recorded with the top gypsy guitarists in the style including Stochelo Rosenberg, Angelo Debarre, Samson Schmitt and Fapy Lafertin.

Not content to stay in the tradition of the 1930s, Tim has released the genre-crossing CD "Rock Django" (2012) with Dutch Sinti guitarist Paulus Schäfer, featuring Django-style renditions of guitar rock classics.

With his own Tim Kliphuis Trio, he performs music from jazz, classical and folk genres leading to invitations for prestigious events such as the Amsterdam Princes Canal's Concert, the Paradiso concert with the Netherlands Chamber Orchestra and hosting Celtic Connections' World Fiddle Night.

As the world's foremost tutor of Gypsy Jazz Violin, Tim gives dozens of workshops every year to violinists with backgrounds in jazz, folk or classical music, in various countries including the UK, Germany, America and South Africa.

In 2010, Tim started Europe's first Grappelli Camp, an annual camp dedicated to gypsy jazz, based in the Netherlands, for violins, guitars and double basses which has grown every year.

He has written the best-selling Mel Bay book "Stéphane Grappelli - Gypsy Jazz Violin" (2008). This was followed by "Hot Jazz Violin" DVDs Volume 1 & 2 (HyperHip Media, 2009) and numerous download videos including Jazz Violin Etudes and Harmony & Accompaniment lessons (DC Music School, 2011). "Grappelli Licks" (Lowland, 2012) is Tim's second book release.

All the above products can be ordered from **www.stephanegrappelli.com**.

For more information about the author, including concert and workshop listings and press photos, please go to **www.timkliphuis.com**.

ACKNOWLEDGEMENTS

My gratitude goes out to all those who helped me write this book. In particular, I would like to thank Stéphanie for the use of her beautiful painting, Charles, Mike and Raymond for their tips, Marc for his proofreading, my students for all their helpful suggestions (it was impossible to realise all of them but I've done my best!), Janneke for her support and last, but not least, Stéphane Grappelli for his inspiring music.

HOW TO USE THIS BOOK

I have tried to make this book as easy to use as possible. It is about licks (short phrases), but also about where and how to play these in your solo chorus. It is also about the gypsy jazz repertoire - what you learn here can be used on all the standards when you're doing a gypsy jam session.

If you are new to this style, or need to refresh your memory, please go through the Getting Started section. It tells you something about the gypsy jazz violin sound, gives you some bowing patterns and shows the rhythmical patterns that you should know.

The chapter on Universal licks shows you some licks that you can use in many different keys. They are simple and quickly learnt - don't miss this one! The 'Using your licks' chapter then explains how to put them into practise.

The next chapters have licks by key, or tonality, in all the common gypsy jazz keys. These are followed by a transcribed playalong solo on a song with some of the licks in it, so you can see how they work 'live'. The playalong solos are on the audio, followed by a longer backing track for you to practise on. The audio backing tracks are played by one of the world's top gypsy guitarists, Paulus Schäfer.

Also on the audio are some of the licks that are not in the playalong solos. I have included the track numbers so you can find them easily.

I discuss a lot of notes, chords and keys in this book. To keep them apart, I have used lower case for notes ('g'), upper case for keys ('Gm' or 'G minor') and italic upper case for chords ('*Gm*' and '*D7*').

In between the chapters, I throw in four short 'Tips', which help you to understand more about how to use your licks.

You can find all the recordings I have used online. In total I discuss around 30 classic Grappelli tracks in this book. If you want to hear all the original licks (not just the ones I play on the audio) go and buy the original recordings on Amazon or iTunes.

What you learn from this book should be a starting point to find your own style. Learn from other jazz greats such as Stan Getz, Joe Pass and Jean-Luc Ponty. Listen to what you like, and make it your own. That way, you create a personal style.

Did you play bluegrass, folk or classical in the past? Don't through those licks away, use them in your solos! It makes it all the more interesting.

GETTING STARTED

Bowing

There is one particular bowing pattern that I want you to practise and make your own. It is at the heart of most of Grappelli's solos. I call it 'jazz bowing' and it is a syncopated bowing, which means it goes against the beat. The 2nd, 5th etc. notes are longer.

Play the following line, using a small amount of bowing in the top half of the bow:

Use a metronome if you need it. When you've got this bowing sorted out, add accents on the longer, off-beat notes. Make the accents light, don't use any more bowing than you had in the example above. Just pinch the bow lightly with your right-hand index finger to make the accents:

Track 20

I would like to do away with a persistent myth about eighth notes (the English call them quavers). Many tuition books and jazz teachers tell you that jazz eighths should be 'swung' like triplets:

Well, sorry to break the news ... but if you want to play medium or up-tempo gypsy jazz, this is wrong. Some American jazz styles have a heavy triplet feel but not the lighter, European gypsy swing. Please read the eighth notes as *straight*. Think of J.S. Bach!

Now practise the jazz bowing pattern on some simple notes (lightly and with a small amount of bow on the top half, no triplets!). The *slurs* glue notes together, in this case two at a time, on one bow, on the first and third off-beat notes:

Now don't forget to add those (light, finger-pinching) accents:

Practice this bowing pattern, with its change of 'up' and 'down' bows per half bar on any notes you like - a simple eighth note scale or something with more string changes, like an arpeggio:

Track 21

This pattern of two slurred, two separate notes can also be played the other way round, with the slur on the second and fourth off-beat notes:

Remember to practise it straight, otherwise you will never be able to play the faster licks, and there are a few of those in this book! Make your own exercises, using other notes, to get familiar with the jazz bowing.

Syncopation

Bowing and syncopation are closely linked. When you are slurring two or more notes in a solo, you are creating a rhythm with the bow. A jazz slur often starts on an off-beat note, which makes it syncopated, giving it swing.

Here is a useful exercise to practise syncopation with the bow. Start with the following pattern (straight eights, no swinging) and repeat it:

Use very little bow, relax, and make the accents with a pinch of your right hand index finger. Play it as often as needed to get comfortable with it, then move to the following rhythm:

Make sure you still feel the beats (=accents), don't turn the rhythm back to the previous example. Keep repeating until it works. When you've done that, you're ready for some syncopation:

And a bit more difficult:

Use the accent to keep track of where the beat is. Play with a metronome, otherwise you'll get confused. Repeat, repeat.

Ghost notes

Now we'll get a little bit more advanced: the real swinging licks often have one or two notes that are played only very softly, so it's more about moving the bow than hearing the note. The real reason is to make the timing of the bow better, but it's also a great sounding jazz trick that gives your solo dynamics and class.

Here are four bars from the theme of Django Reinhardt's Belleville in D - there is syncopation but also a ghost note on the second b♭ in bars 2 and 4:

Track 22

You see the ghost note is written between brackets. Practise it like this:

Play the open D string so softly that you can't really hear it. Take the pressure off the bow by lifting it slightly, without it leaving the string.

Now try this one (you can make your own exercises with ghost notes, just pick a line of notes and decided which ones to 'ghost'):

Here are two open string ghost notes in a typical lick - play them so that you see the bow move, but you don't hear the open string at all:

Track 23

The ghost notes above are called *separate* ghost notes. There is also a second type of ghost note, which is a *slurred* ghost note. It is connected to a regular note with a slur. In the example below, lift the pressure off the bow halfway the slur (like a very fast diminuendo) to ghost the open string:

Track 24

You shouldn't hear the open D string at all really. Here is another one:

Again, you play the open strings much softer than the fourth and third fingers. This is what it should sound like:

You can come back to this later, when you've seen some ghost notes in action in the upcoming chapters. Now it's time to look at some theory and then start learning some Grappelli licks!

BASIC CHORD THEORY

When you take a song, the first thing to find out is its key. For instance, with the song Coquette, the key is D. That means you can play licks in D major on it. However, you can't play every lick all the time. That is because the song has different chords.

Most chords in a song are *diatonic*. That means they made with notes from the D major scale (d, e, f♯, g, a, b and c♯). Here I have written all diatonic chords in D, using four note arpeggios everywhere. Below the chords are their steps:

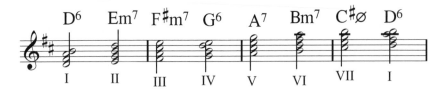

Looking at the notes of the chords, you can see that there is a lot of overlap between different steps. This makes it much simpler for us - we just find the steps that are related and bunch them together in a group.

Step I (the 'I') is called the Tonic. If you look carefully, you'll discover that the VI has exactly the same notes, but with a different one at the bottom. The III is also related, with 2 common notes or even 3 if we play a major 7th (c♯) on the D chord instead of a 6th (b). So let's bunch the I, the III and the VI together in the *Tonic* group.

The V is called the Dominant. It dominates the Tonic because it wants to resolve to it, in a harmonic movement called the *cadence* (V-I). Check out the II and you'll see that it has two notes in common with the V, and three if we add a 9th note on the V (b). Then check out the IV and see that it has the same notes as the II. And you might have missed it, but the VII has nearly the same notes as the V!
So we can bunch the II, IV, V and VII together in the *Dominant* group.

That's all the steps bunched into two groups, Tonic and Dominant. Now you can learn two types of licks in the key of D, Tonic and Dominant licks, and you can play on all these chords!

Of course, you can treat the chords separately as Minor or Major chords, and the VII is a special chord called Half diminished, on which diminished licks can be played. How to do all this will be shown in the book, but as long as you simplify things for yourself a bit, you don't need to learn large amounts of chord theory to improvise a nice solo.

That is the theory in a nutshell, but you need another very important thing: your ears. They will tell you what sounds good and what sounds bad. Let your ears lead you in anything you play, and don't ignore them: they are usually right!

UNIVERSAL LICKS

What is a 'lick'? I use the word to describe a catchy melodic or rhythmic phrase that is not too long, and that is used more than once, on different solos. In other words, a small building block for soloing. Like LEGO.

When you are stuck in a solo, you grab a lick that comes to mind and play it right there. It helps you sound more 'professional' and gives you extra soloing material. You shouldn't play only licks, because then you don't sound like yourself. So you mix them in with your own notes.

Here are some licks that you can play in lots of different keys. They are simple to learn and effective. I call them Universal licks.

The '9' lick

Here is the '9' lick - the best-known jazz lick in the world. Everybody uses it, even players like John Coltrane. Let's have a closer look:

This lick makes good use of the open strings - you can go to third position after the open D string but in this key you can also stay in first position. Use it on any *G major* chord (for example, the start of Lady Be Good).

This lick can be played downwards as well as upwards, like this:

Track 25

In minor, it sounds just as good. Here is the same lick, same fingering, in G minor (for example, the song Minor Blues). Again, you can change position, but staying in first position works too):

You can transpose this lick to a number of keys that sound great. Try to keep at least one open string in there, so you can do the position change if needed. Let's try D (Coquette):

... and Dm (I've Found A New Baby); both of these need the position change to make it up to the top notes.

To finish, how about Am (Minor Swing), up and down:

Etcetera. Make yourself comfortable with this lick as you will be using it a lot. Practice it in the keys of the songs you are playing, at different speeds. Use a metronome if you like.

The Pentatonic lick

Using the '9' major lick, you can add one note, the major 6th, to make it a Pentatonic lick. This means that the arpeggio you play is made up of five notes. In G major:

And another one:

You could also say that this arpeggio is a major scale with the 4th and 7th notes left out. Let's look at the full G major pentatonic scale:

Track 26

Interestingly, the pentatonic is a scale as well as an arpeggio with five notes, depending on how you see it. It bridges the gap between the two.

There is another bridge: pentatonic material connects relative major and minor keys, which you will read more about in Tip #1: *Playing Minor on Major Chords* (page 37). Pentatonic sounds like major and minor at the same time, and can be used on a lot of different chords. A great help if you're not sure of what you're doing!

As you can see, E minor pentatonic uses the same notes as G major pentatonic.

There is also a Blues Pentatonic scale, but it is not the right time to explain that one yet. It works on the same principle, but with different scale notes and some alterations. Read about Blue notes, and find the Blues Pentatonic discussed in Tip #4: *Blue Notes* (page 70).

Arpeggiated melodies

There are some universally used licks which are melodies built round the arpeggio notes. They sound a bit more melodic than the examples above, and yet are very simple to make.

The first example is in C, using the arpeggio steps c, g and e. The bowing is suggested but please try your own bowing - avoid using the same bowing on every group of notes, as that makes it sound a bit boring.

Using the above example, but turning it round (going up instead of down), I have also added some upwards leading chromatic notes: $d\sharp$ and $f\sharp$.

Another variant, using the downward leading notes only:

And here a lick with some downwards leading *chromatic* notes - $d\flat$ and $a\flat$:

The following is a typical Grappelli trick that you hear a lot. It has triplet eights (quite fast! Practice with a metronome and accent only the first note of the triplet) and uses the chromatic sound from the example above.

Track 27

You can make your own arpeggiated melodies by changing these examples a bit. Here is what you could do with the lick above, playing it the key of G:

I have changed the middle notes (up instead of down).

Practice these licks in different keys, major and minor. They come in handy when you need to fill some time in a solo before coming up with a really cool lick, or if you want to change the register (go from low to high on the instrument or the other way round).

The Dominant lick

Now let's get back to the key of G. The dominant of G is *D7*. If you are not sure what a dominant is, I refer you to the Basic Chord Theory chapter (page 10).

A dominant chord sounds special because it has a minor 7th. When playing a dominant chord, it is a good idea to accent this in the lick. Grappelli uses a nice phrase where he combines the major 7th, the minor 7th, the major 9th and minor 9th in a chromatic way. This lick can be used on many different keys, and it is one of his favourite licks.

Do the same in the key of C, where the dominant is *G7*:

Or the key of B♭, where the dominant is *F7* (play an open E string, it sounds great that way - this is the basis for all chromatic fingering, more about this in Tip #2 - Chromatic Notes, on page 50):

And so on. It really works on all keys and as the dominant pops up everywhere, it's a great lick to have in your repertoire. Practice it in the other major gypsy jazz keys as well (D, F and A), and make yourself comfortable with the bowing.

The Chromatic Dominant lick

The chromatic dominant lick takes the idea of using major and minor 7th, and extends it a bit by including the minor and major 3rd. Try this on G major, using the suggested fingering (2-2 is a rhythmical slide from one note to the other):

Major and minor 7th are c♯ and c, minor and major 3rd are f and f♯. This pattern can be extended if the dominant is not one, but two bars ...

... or even longer if you want. It sounds great in D major too, nice and bright as you're on the E and A strings. Here is a long version in D (so the dominant is *A7*). Use the same fingering.

The Honeysuckle Rose Dominant lick

Do you know the Fats Waller standard Honeysuckle Rose? The melody, which is really an up-and-down arpeggio, is catchy and simple, and it is based on the dominant chord of the song, using the 6th and 9th note of the arpeggio. This melody is perfect for playing on any dominant chord, which makes it another universal dominant lick. Here it is, in G:

Notice there is a ghost note (the one between brackets). Check how to play this note on page 8. The bowing is simple: start with a down bow, no slurs, so you finish up bow on the g. This lick is universal like the ones discussed above, because it can be transposed easily. Try it in the key of F:

When you transpose, sometimes you can choose between different octaves in first position. Here is what I mean - let's transpose the lick to C, so it's played on the *G7* dominant chord. Here is a low version ...

... and here is a high version:

Make yourself familiar with all the universal licks in this way, by transposing them and playing them high or low on the instrument, using as many open strings as possible.

The 'Flat 9' Dominant lick

When you are playing in a minor key, the dominant should be played a bit differently. It has an extra leading note, namely a flat 9th and we want to include this note in the lick. This is what I call the Flat 9 Dominant lick, on *E7* in Am (the flat 9th is the note f):

As before, you can play this universal lick in other keys. For gypsy jazz, the minor keys are Dm, Gm and Cm. Let's see what it looks like in Dm, for example:

And this is the same lick in Gm:

Track 28

Let's go back to Am. Here is a variation on the Flat 9 dominant lick, which I use a lot. It has the same notes as the original Flat 9 lick, but arranged in a different way:

Notice that it does not finish on the root note of the tonic (*Am*). It finishes on the 3rd. If you want to finish on the root note (a), just add a few notes like this:

Here is a version in Cm - transpose the lick into the other keys yourself and make sure you always include the flat 9th (in this case a♭):

The Diminished lick

A small change turns the minor key's dominant lick into a diminished or 'dim' lick. To learn about diminished chords and related theory, please check out my book "Stéphane Grappelli - Gypsy Jazz Violin" (*www.stephanegrappelli.com*). This change is very simple: you just leave out the root note. Let's have a look at an *E7* Diminished lick:

As you see, there is no e in this lick, which would have been the root note for *E7*. By playing the 4 note arpeggio with a flat 9th without the root you are suggesting the dimished chord (*G♯dim*, which has the same dominant function as *E7*). Let's try a different starting note:

The diminished arpeggio is symmetrical: you can start the lick on any of the four notes. Try it - I've shown you those starting on f and g♯, which leaves b and d. See if you can finish on the right note on the *Am* chord too - there should be no jumps.

Of course, you should study this lick in the different minor keys. Here is an example: a diminished lick on the Dominant in the key of Dm (*C♯dim* lick on *A7*):

USING YOUR LICKS

Once you have learnt a lick, the next step is to learn to use it on the songs you play. The original lick is only a building block, and sometimes needs changing to fit into different songs. Or maybe you have to learn where to position the lick in the bar. Here is what you need to do to organise a flexible library of licks for yourself.

Transposing

Unlike many jazz players, Grappelli only used certain licks on certain keys. He rarely transposed his licks except for changes in fifths (moving up or down a string) or changes from major to minor and back. The reason is that on a violin, a good lick uses the open strings and you want it to keep that quality.

What is great about this limited use of licks in different keys, is that every key has its own, particular licks. So every key (and song) sounds different. This is a natural way of keeping the music fresh and new, as long as you play your songs in different keys of course.

What I'd like you to do when you learn a new lick, is to try out if it is transposable to another key without losing its feel. Here is an example in C major:

Transposing down to F major works fine, we still have the open strings:

Transposing to B♭ doesn't work so well, the string changes are impractical this way:

Decide for yourself what works and what doesn't. Be flexible but don't practise licks in all twelve keys. Frankly, it's a waste of time.

Positioning

Where to put a lick you've just learnt? This depends on the chords of the song. For some simple tips, I refer you to Basic Chord Theory on page 10, and my previous book "Stéphane Grappelli - Gypsy Jazz Violin" (*www.stephanegrappelli.com*).

To play the right lick over the right chord, you need to know the following:

- There are only THREE chord families: Major, Minor and Dominant.
- EVERY chord in gypsy jazz belongs to one of these families.
- EVERY lick in this book was made for one of these groups.

I have arranged the licks according to the key of the songs. For instance, D major is the key of Coquette. In the D major chapter, I show you Tonic licks on the *D* chord, and Dominant licks on the *A7* chord.

When you have figured out where the Tonic and Dominant chords are in the song Coquette, you will know where to put your licks. Tonic isn't only the *I* (first step, *D*) but also the *VI* (*Bm7*), for example, as we have seen in the Basic Chord Theory chapter on page 10. Dominant is not only *V* (*A7*) but also *II* (*Em7*), as you will see in Tip #3: Playing Minor on the Dominant, page 61.

The 'bridge' or 'middle eight' is always a bit different, with Tonic and Dominant chords in a different key or keys. For the bridge you go to the chapter of the appropriate key and find the licks you can play there.

This book shows licks in the most popular gypsy jazz keys. In order to have licks for all the chords in all the gypsy jazz songs in the world, you can transpose existing licks into different keys. This way, you can use the idiom of Stéphane Grappelli on any song, anytime.

Timing

Practising the timing of your lick is essential. There are many different ways to time a lick, and they make it sound very different too. That's why timing is a way of bringing variation in your playing, without learning more notes.

Here is a first Grappelli lick from the song It Had To Be You, recorded in London, 1938 as a duet with Django, on which Grappelli switches from piano to violin.

Bowings are suggested. Sometimes it is impossible to hear what exact bowings Grappelli used, and in those cases I have followed his general bowing patterns. Feel free to make your own bowings - you should feel comfortable with them.

This whole lick is in 3rd position. The ghost note ( ) is bowed very lightly so you hardly hear it, see page 9. Every slur starts with a little accent with the right hand, as discussed on page 7. Remember to play straight, not triplets. Otherwise it won't swing!

A great Grappelli trick is to use this lick again but start it on a different beat. Here is an example starting on the first beat:

Track 30

It's the same lick, but sounds very different. Good, hey? You can use this principle on all licks, with great results.

Here is a longer It Had To Be You lick, which also starts with an upbeat. Again, watch your accents and ghost notes, and straight timing.

Track 31

This lick could start on a different beat too. How about this:

Track 32

So you see, if you are creative with the timing in this way, you don't need very many notes to have a lot of different sounding licks! Try this out with the licks in the book and you will have a flexible repertoire. Licks are building blocks, you can use them any way you want.

There is not enough space on the CD to play you every lick separately, so a lot of the licks are played in the sample solos. The rest can be found on the recordings mentioned at the beginning of the chapters.

From now on, I assume that you know every slur should start with a small accent. So I won't be writing accents on the slurs anymore. You can hear them on the samples on the CD. Make it a habit to play an accent on the start of every slur.

LICKS IN G

Let's now have look at how Grappelli uses his other, personal licks on songs in specific keys. I've selected some great licks for you to practice. We'll start with songs in G major and then move on to other major and minor keys, concentrating on the songs that Grappelli played a lot.

I have taken the licks in this chapter from the following recordings in G:

- Limehouse Blues (1935, Paris) - Quintette of the Hot Club of France
- It Had To Be You (1938, London) - Django Reinhardt & Stéphane Grappelli
- How High the Moon (1947, Rome) - Django Reinhardt & Stéphane Grappelli
- Limehouse Blues (1972, London) - Barney Kessel & Stéphane Grappelli
- Lady Be Good (1972, London) - Stéphane Grappelli Live
- Pent-Up House (1981, Boston) - Stéphane Grappelli & David Grisman Live
- Tiger Rag (1981, Boston) - Stéphane Grappelli & David Grisman Live

To get into the right feel, why not find these and the other recordings in this book online or on vinyl or cd, and listen to the licks that way. It's important to search for the right year, as Grappelli recorded most songs many times!

Tonic (*G*) licks

In his improvisation on It Had To Be You, Grappelli plays a straightforward arpeggio lick using the major 7th note (f♯) as part of the chord. It sounds like this:

As we saw before in the Universal Licks chapter, the arpeggio plays an important role in making up licks. More important, I would say, than the scale. The jumps between notes somehow give it a swingy character that fits the style.

Right at the start of the song, Grappelli plays a great lick using the raised 4th (c♯) which gives it a very jazzy sound. Notice the upbeat, and the position change at the end, sliding the second finger up:

On the Quintette's Limehouse Blues recording, there is another good example of fast arpeggio playing, using the major 7th note (f#) again:

At the end of Grappelli's How High the Moon solo, there is a partly syncopated line which could have been played by Louis Armstrong, it is so simple and swinging:

Here another line which has a lot of altered notes in third position, with a long upbeat. Check the bowing, it works very well like that:

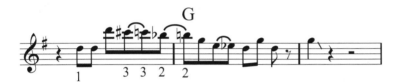

This is a lick which you can time differently - let's bring the beat forward, like this, and you see it still works:

On his incredible Lady Be Good recording, live with piano, bass and drums, Grappelli plays the more bluesy notes that I talk about in this book (in this case, the note b♭, which is the flat 3rd):

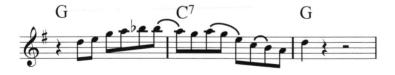

Similarly, using both b♭ and b, and the raised 4th (c#), he plays:

Here's another catchy lick from the same recording, which can be used on any fast tune, and is very easily transposed to a different key. Third position, double stopping with the open E string and holding the fourth finger on the high g on the A string:

On Pent-Up House, live with David Grisman, he uses the blue note f often. Here is an example with f and b♭:

Notice how in his later period, Grappelli plays much less slurred on the fast songs than in the thirties, as this broken scale lick will show - try it yourself on a fast tempo, with very little bow and you will feel that it works:

The same but going down from the E string (notice the raised 4th again):

In third position, here is a great one, syncopated and slurred, that you can use in many keys, varying the top notes any way you like:

To finish, here is a nice trick on the E string involving the 6th note (e) harmonic. You play the high "0" note (top e) by lightly resting the fourth finger on the string, without pressing down.

Track 33

24

Dominant (*D7*) Licks

From Django and Stéphane's duet version of It Had To Be You comes the following dominant lick (*D7* is the dominant in G) at the end of the song. Play the first three notes with one finger, sliding slowly but rhythmically from a to b♭ and back. The slur over the barline makes for an interesting syncopated rhythm:

With the dominant, the *V* (*D7*) is often preceded by *II* (*Am7*). They are slightly different chords but have the same dominant function - see also Tip #3: Playing Minor on the Dominant, page 61. You can use your dominant licks on both. Here is a lick from the Hot Club Quintette's Limehouse Blues, at the end of Grappelli's first solo. Notice it starts after a two beat rest, and check out the use of the 6th (the note b) on *D7* - Grappelli did that a lot.

Another one from this recording, starting a beat into the dominant bar, in 3rd position:

Or, from the fun live recording of Pent-Up House with the David Grisman Quintet later in Grappelli's career, two similar *II-V-I* sequences with a few chromatic notes thrown in at the end, starting half a bar before the *Am7* chord:

and

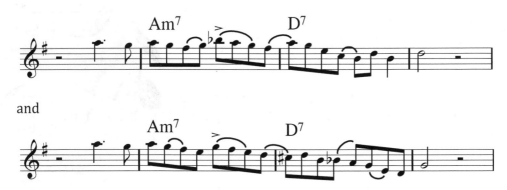

All right, I'll sneak in another one with the same ending, but a different start, from the same concert, on the song Tiger Rag:

Track 34

This is typical of Grappelli's fast songs. His licks have a few small variations but rely on roughly the same pattern and bowings. This way he manages to stay very relaxed at very high tempos.

Here is a more bluesy approach to the dominant, taken from the live version of Lady Be Good, in concert in 1971:

Normally speaking it's not a good idea to play a flat 3rd (f) on the dominant (D7) but this lick works because of its bluesy sound, and Grappelli uses it often. Make sure you ghost the open D string twice in the second bar, lifting pressure off the bow after playing the start of the slurs (f).

A similar thing can be heard on It Had To Be You, with the same use of the f. Watch the syncopated upbeat!

The next lick, taken from the Limehouse Blues recording with guitarist Barney Kessel (one of Grappelli's best albums!) combines this bluesy sound with a more modern-sounding alteration on the flat 9th, only to finish safely on the dominant's root, the note d. Watch the accents in the second bar, you really need to highlight the beats and make the off-beats a bit softer:

Track 35

Here's a nice one from the Rome recording of How High the Moon, right at the end of Stéphanes statement of the theme:

The chromatic notes 1-1 are slides, like before, and the first slur with the accent should get softer towards the end, leaving the note 'a' very soft, like a ghost note. The triplet might seem tricky but is easy enough if you practice it exactly in time, a bit slower, with a metronome.

Another possibility on a *II-V-I* (in this case, *Am7-D7-G*) is to make the *II*, *Am7*, a dominant chord (*A7*, with a c$\sharp$) on your solo. This is called an alteration: the melody suggests a slightly different chord than the rhythm section are playing. Grappelli does this often. Here is an example where he also adds a flat 9th (b$\flat$) to the altered chord, on Lady Be Good:

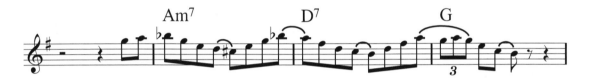

Playalong solo on the chords of "It Had To Be You" (G)

Here is a sample solo on the song It Had To Be You. The form is AA, 32 bars total. I have included Tonic and Dominant licks from G major, transposed licks from other keys, Universal licks and some new licks. I have annotated page numbers and the number of the lick on the page, for you to check back: *"p. 79 - 3"* means it is the 3ⁿᵈ lick discussed on page 79. Notice that I sometimes start or finish a lick differently, or use only a little bit of it, or change the bowing, depending on the situation. That's allowed!

Track 2

Track 3 is a longer backing track for you to try your own solos and licks out - you are playing to the rhythm guitar of gypsy guitarist Paulus Schäfer.

Track 3

28

LICKS IN C

The next key we'll look at is C major. It is as widely used as G in gypsy jazz, and it swings great. No sharps, no flats. You can still use all the open violin strings G, D, A and E a lot, which makes it an easy key to improvise in.

I have taken the licks in C from the following recordings:

- Shine (1937, Paris) - Quintette of the Hot Club of France
- Exactly Like You (1937, Paris) - Quintette of the Hot Club of France
- I Saw Stars (1947, Rome) - Django Reinhardt & Stéphane Grappelli
- Swing 42 (1949, Rome) - Django Reinhardt & Stéphane Grappelli
- Shine (1981, Boston) - Stéphane Grappelli & David Grisman Live
- Swing 42 (1982, Saratoga, CA) - Stéphane Grappelli Live

Tonic (*C*) licks

Here is a great sounding lick from the 1937 Shine, which Stéphane Grappelli plays at the end of the theme, before the singer starts:

The thing about this lick is that it has not just the chord notes of the chord *C* (c, e, g) but two additions as well: the 6th note (a) and the 9th note (d). These five notes together are called the pentatonic scale, which you find discussed in the Universal Licks section, on page 12.

A more bluesy tonic lick in Grappelli's solo goes like this:

Note the double slide from d to e♭ and back, with one finger. I call this a push-pull. The blue note e♭ gives it a great sound. This lick is used by Grappelli in A minor a lot too. Check out the A minor licks in this book and you'll find it there as well. The relationship between C major and A minor is that of the relative minor: the two chords are related (they are basically the same chord!). Check Tip #1: Playing Minor on Major Chords, page 37 to read more about this.

Another one, from Django and Stéphane's version of I Saw Stars, starts the same but goes on a little bit longer:

Here is a lick from Shine again, going up, with a chromatic sound, starting after the beat, that can be used both on the tonic (*C*) or dominant (*G7*) chord:

The reason it works on a *G7* chord too, is because the g and the f (both notes of that chord) are important notes in this lick. Grappelli plays it twice at the end of his solo, on *C* and then on *G7*, and it sounds great.

The I Saw Stars version of this lick is slightly different, starting a third up but using the same material:

Here is a lick for the E string. Another push-pull, the same notes d-e♭-d but an octave up. This fingering is used a lot, in C major but also in A minor (e.g. Minor Swing, check out the example on page 38).

Track 36

This is one of those licks that Grappelli used in many different contexts, on different songs, and timed differently as well. As an example, you could start it on the first beat, instead of the third:

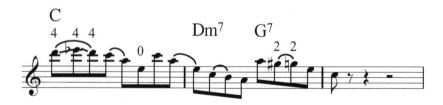

30

A more fun and simple group of four notes uses the fingering 2-1-1-0 on A and E strings, and it can be played slow or double speed (with only three notes in the group). This is what Grappelli does with it on I Saw Stars:

Here, from the modern Shine recording with Grisman, is a similar pattern that can be repeated as often as you like. It uses the 6th note (a):

Notice that the bowing of the six notes stays the same, so the rhythm goes across the bar and against the beat, making it sound like a 3/4 measure. You can make it longer:

Further on in his solo, Grappelli plays a variant of this one, which fills a whole bar (not just three beats):

A similar line occurs on his statement of the theme in the Quintette's recording of Exactly Like You (notice the old-fashioned use of continuous off-beat slurs) with a nice bluesy sound:

Here is a really melodious lick, in the middle of the Shine solo, for a change after all those many fast notes, and it's a catchy melody which goes as follows:

You see that some tonic licks spill over into the dominant, *G7* chord. It doesn't always work and depends on the notes you are using. Let your ears tell you if it sounds allright. If it doesn't, time the lick earlier so that it stops before the barline where the change of harmony happens.

Here is another 'simple' lick which is inspired by the notes of Jerome Kern's Ol' Man River, played by Grappelli on his modern live recording of Swing 42 at the beginning of his solo:

Track 37

In the Universal Licks chapter, we looked at melodies based round the arpeggio. When Grappelli plays in C major, he often adds the note f$\sharp$ (the raised 4th as seen before in G major) to add some spice to his sound. This is one of his most prominent licks in C from his later period in the seventies and eighties:

These last two licks are very easy to use in other keys as well. See if you can transpose them to, say, D major, G major and F major?

Here is a combination of the f$\sharp$, an added b$\flat$ and the repeated 6th lick from earlier on. These kind of combinations make Grappelli's idiom sound endless, when in fact he uses very few motifs. He just combines them in a very creative way:

Another chromatic note can be found in the Swing 42 recording, this time it's a g♯:

And on this song, Grappelli plays the E string lick again, but without the first note, and timed as follows:

Dominant (G7) licks

From Grappelli's improvisation on the Quintette's 'Shine' recording, here is a dominant lick used three times. It is the arpeggio of dominant chord *G7*, with a 9th note added. Notice that it starts with an upbeat:

This lick would be hard to transpose to a different key as it crosses all the strings, from top to bottom. It is typically used in C only.

A variation on this lick occurs a third time in the solo - this time the upbeat is placed on the first beat of the bar and the lick has been shortened, ending on a different note. This trick of changing the timing is exactly what we looked at before. See how it works:

Because this is a shorter lick not using all the strings, you can easily transpose it a fifth down. It then becomes a *C7* dominant lick in the key of F. Try it:

That was just to remind you that you can transpose some licks to different keys, and use them on different tunes. Keep trying this when you learn a new lick, to see how it sounds in another key.

On Grappelli's modern, live, Swing 42 recording, as the Dominant cadences are not just *G7-C* but *Dm7-G7-C*, you can hear him suggesting more of the *Dm7* chord than in the thirties recordings with the Quintette (the 'o' means that the note is the first G string harmonic, use the third or fourth finger for that):

A dominant lick going up, instead of down, can be heard on Exactly Like You. At the start, the flat 9th (a♭) adds a distinct colour:

On his theme in I Saw Stars, Grappelli plays a lick made totally out of arpeggio material, without any altered notes (do you recognize the '9' lick from the Universal Licks chapter?):

And in his solo, a combination of chromatic and arpeggiated runs (using that slurred bowing of his early period):

Syncopation plays an important role in Grappelli's solos, also on the early Swing 42 recording. Remember, *Dm7* and *G7* are both Dominant in function, resolving to *C*. This upbeat is hard to play, it's so syncopated:

And finally, here is a longer version using the third finger slide that Grappelli made famous. Look where the open strings are and play them that way, followed by the slide. Again, this syncopated upbeat:

Track 38

Playalong solo on the chords of "Shine" (C)

Here is a sample solo on Shine. The form is AA, 32 bars. As with the other solos, I've taken licks from all parts of the book. I have annotated the page number and the number of the lick: *"p. 32 - 1"* means the 1st lick discussed on page 32.

If you are new to the melody of this song, please look it up online or find one of the recordings mentioned at the beginning of this C major chapter, and learn it.

Track 4

Use **Track 5** to practice your licks with guitar chords only.

Track 5

TIP #1: PLAYING MINOR ON MAJOR CHORDS

In jazz, the minor licks somehow sound 'cooler' than the major licks. As most songs are in major keys, there's not much chance to play them. A way to get round this, is to play our cool minor licks on major songs, using a trick called Minor on Major.

What you do is, you take the major chord (let's say, C) and then go down a minor 3rd, to its relative minor (Am). Relative minor means that C and Am have the same scale notes, and their chords are related. Compare the C6 chord with Am7:

They are exactly the same chord, with a different note at the bottom. So you can play an A minor lick on the C chord:

The note 'a' is the 6th note on C, a perfectly acceptable sound. Now let's see how Grappelli uses this principle. Remember this lick? The notes he plays are those of Am, with a flat 5th thrown in (e^b). You will find similar lines in the next chapter:

You can take it a bit further by adding the major 6th in Am, f#, which is not a scale note in C major (but we've seen it before as a raised 4th). It adds an interesting colour:

Now put all this into practice: some licks from the Am chapter might be perfect for soloing in C major, licks from the Dm chapter could work well in F, and Gm licks could be useful for B^b. The three minor chapters in this book all have their relative major key. Try it out for yourself and let your ears decide what works and what doesn't.

LICKS IN A minor

There are not many songs in A minor in gypsy jazz. However, the most famous gypsy jazz song of all time, Minor Swing, is in this key so there's a good reason to discuss it. And Grappelli played one or two other songs in A minor too.

I have taken the licks from the following recordings:

- Minor Swing (1937, Paris) - Quintette of the Hot Club of France
- Minor Swing (1962, Paris) - Stéphane Grappelli Quintet
- You'd Be So Nice To Come Home To (1975-76, Paris) - Grappelli plays Cole Porter

Tonic (*Am*) licks

Let's start with the famous 1937 Minor Swing solo, a Grappelli classic. I have transcribed and explained the whole solo in my book "Stéphane Grappelli - Gypsy Jazz Violin" (*www.stephanegrappelli.com*) but will highlight a few useful Tonic licks right here, starting with:

Notice the major 7th, g♯, which confirms the minor feel (it is the leading note in A minor). The ghost note is an open E string, after which you change position on the E string, ending on a harmonic with a stretched fourth finger.

A more riff-like motif is found at the start of Stéphane's third solo chorus:

That was a focus on the third note (c). But the fourth note, d, works quite well on A minor too. It is followed by the c, so it resolves downward:

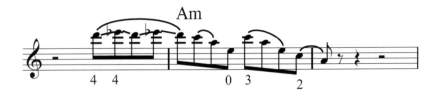

38

A syncopated start, followed by the bluesy flat 5th, the e♭: on a major key the bluesy note would be a flat 3rd, but in minor it is already there so the 5th is the next blue note option. Refer to Tip #4: Blue notes, page 70 for more info on how this works.

And a slight variation (see how often Grappelli repeats himself? Yet always a little bit differently, so it never sounds the same):

Look at the rhythm on the final bar on both these licks: two eighth notes followed by two quarter notes, of which the first one is shortened to an eighth's length. You will find this rhythm in Grappelli's solos a lot, at the end of a phrase. As if he is saying: that is that.

Let's now look at a later, but no less brilliant solo on Minor Swing, recorded in 1962 with a studio band on one of his best albums "Feeling + Finesse = Jazz". This solo goes on for seven whole choruses, with some counterpoint playing against double bass lines at the end. Here is a first lick.

He is flying - look at the use of his bowing (fewer slurs than in the old days, just slurring two notes together here and there) and the chromatic run, starting and finishing on the root note (a) is timed beautifully to finish on the downbeat. The fingering reminds you how you should play these chromatic notes, and for more details check Tip #2: Chromatic Notes on page 50.

Same start, bluesy finish:

And a really syncopated figure (this goes on for longer on the recording):

The interesting thing is that in the sixties and seventies, which was his best period, Grappelli sounds much freer than in the old Quintette days. One of the reasons, as I said earlier, had to do with noise levels: softer bands and better amplification gave him the chance to play more relaxed. But he was also a better and more complete player - sometimes playing almost too many notes, but just in time going back to a very simple and effective motif to give our ears a rest. He had a natural genius for balance in his solos, something we all should aim for!

A medium tempo song in A minor is Cole Porter's You'd Be So Nice To Come Home To. Interestingly, this is in two keys, starting out in A minor but finishing on C major, the major parallel - just what I was talking about in Tip #1 (page 37).

Here is a Tonic lick on that song - the tempo is slower than Minor Swing so Grappelli manages to throw in a sixteenth run, combining a version of the riff-like motif above with the bluesy endings from Minor Swing. Don't worry about the Bm chord, it is a passing chord within Am as you can see from the solo:

Track 39

Dominant ($E7^{\flat}9$) licks

On a minor key (we're in A minor), the Dominant chord has an important addition: the flat 9th. This is one of the leading notes in the scale of the Tonic. On *E7*, the flat 9th is the note f.

E7 also has a g♯ (its 3rd) so there is a wide gap between these two notes. Try playing them - this gap gives things a harmonic sound, which is perfect for gypsy jazz. If you want to know the scale, it is called, not surprisingly, the harmonic scale:

Grappelli's Dominant licks in A minor, as you will see, have this combination of notes. The clearest example is from the Quintette's famous Minor Swing recording, right at the start of his solo:

The second bar features the arpeggio of *E7* with its flat 9th. Here is another lick which has the 7th and 9th in the first bar, followed by the bluesy push-pull that we've seen in the C major chapter (remember, C major and A minor are parallels - you can use certain phrases on both keys):

It is also possible to play g instead of g♯. This sounds a bit more modern. It only really works on a downward moving line, as if the g is a downward leading note. Here is an example on Grappelli's 1962 Minor Swing, again a very chromatic one, but ending on the traditional harmonic sound from the licks above:

And here's a nice combination of sharp and flat 9th notes, played in a syncopated way, later in the same solo:

To finish, here is an example on the slower You'd Be So Nice... This Dominant features a *II-V-I* cadence. As we saw, the *V* in A major is *E7♭9* with a flat 9th note, f. This same f is a flat 5th on the *II*, *Bm7*, making the chord half diminished. We write this down as *Bm7♭5*. Still there? Check out this lick on *II-V*, Grappelli plays the half dimished arpeggio for you to see:

A typical off-beat Grappelli bowing: slur, two separate, slur, two separate, etc. This pattern should look pretty familiar by now. If not, revisit the Bowing chapter on page 6 to refresh your memory.

Playalong solo on the chords of "Minor Swing" (Am)

Here is a sample solo on Minor Swing. If you don't know the song yet, listen to the original 1937 recording as mentioned at the beginning of this chapter. Minor Swing is only 16 bars long, so I have played the licks over two choruses (32 bars). Remember it is a sample solo made up of licks from the book - when you solo, combine these licks with your own notes.

Practice with **Track 7** - it has eight choruses of guitar chords.

Track 7

LICKS IN D

Time for another popular key: D major. Not normally a jazz key, D might not be very helpful at a regular jazz jam session. In gypsy jazz, however, it is very popular. Django and Stéphane used the key a lot, for songs like Coquette, Daphne, Belleville, Them There Eyes and more.

Use the violin's open strings as much as you can, and you'll notice you can play in a very relaxed way in D major. Relaxed means swinging!

I discussed the most popular song in D, Daphne, in my previous book. I have decided not to revisit it as you can read about it there. The recordings I have used here are:

- Coquette (1946, London) - Quintette of the Hot Club of France
- Belleville (1946, London) - Quintette of the Hot Club of France
- It's Only a Paper Moon (1972, London) - Stéphane Grappelli & Barney Kessel
- Blue Moon (1990, Australia) - Stéphane Grappelli Live

Tonic (*D*) licks

The key of D is a great one for blue notes. To learn more about them, check Tip #4: Blue Notes on page 70. Here is a typical example in third position, played on the Belleville recording when Django and Stéphane recorded together again in London after the war. The minor 7th (c) and flat 5th (a♭), and a suggestion of flat 3rd (f) through the slide - all the blue notes are there:

Or, a bit longer and with an upbeat line, but basically the same lick, nearly fifty years later on Blue Moon (live in Australia with the Grappelli Trio):

Notice that both lines go down after the slides - bluesy lines don't often go up, as the blue notes naturally lead downwards. Some more chromatic notes, including the flat 3rd, are found in this one:

Track 41

(See all those *Em7* and *A7* chords? Blue Moon and Belleville have "rhythm changes" which switch back and forth between the Tonic and a short Dominant cadence. When you play these short changes, you generally play Tonic lines only).

Grappelli's later, more modern style includes a lot of bluesy licks. Here is an example from Blue Moon again, with a minor 7th, flat 5th and flat 6th (b^b):

Take the middle riff from the example above and you can repeat that on the chord of *D*. It works like a charm:

On Coquette, from the London sessions again, Grappelli plays a lick starting with the 9th note (e) and featuring the major 7th note (c$\sharp$) as follows (no blue notes here!):

On downward lines, Grappelli often throws in the 4th note (g) as a leading note to the 3rd. This is what it sounds like, a very useful lick in different keys - try it out:

This lick can also be played over two octaves, and then it helps you come down from high up on the E string - don't shift position until you've played an open A string, then come down:

I like this lick very much and to me it feels a bit like a Universal lick, as I play it often and in all different keys. Just to remind you about transposing your licks, here is a transposed version in B♭:

Another diatonic lick (without chromatic notes) uses the 6th note (b), again on the live Blue Moon recording. Play the quarter notes long and groovy:

Like it more syncopated? Here's a great one from Paper Moon:

Dominant (A7) licks

The dominant of D is A7: a, c♯,e , g. There are some great licks on A7 - Grappelli likes to use chromatic, leading notes into the arpeggio notes as follows, in the improvisation on Coquette:

Notice that the arpeggio above is really an *E minor 7th* arpeggio (e, g, b, d). *Em7* is related to A7 (they are *II* and *V* in D major) as will be discussed in Tip #3: Playing Minor on the Dominant, page 61. This trick of using a minor on the dominant is very useful as it gives you twice as many licks to use on the dominant chord. Here is another one, in the next bars of Coquette:

You see that there is an *Em7* chord in the first bar, but the E minor lick doesn't get played until the second bar, on *A7*. This is called *delaying* - your lick is far more interesting if it not played exactly in the bar it was made for.

Here is another E minor lick on *A7*, borrowed from It Had To Be You in the G major chapter - the notes played are those of *Em6* (e, g, b, c♯):

And now a bluesy one from Paper Moon. The first note is the 3rd position harmonic with the stretched fourth finger, followed by a push-pull with the fourth, still in third position. The blue notes are the flat 5th and flat 3rd of *D* (a♭ and f):

Track 42

On the *A7*, Grappelli plays a bluesy *D* lick. How does that work? Well, only because in the next bar, the *A7* resolves to D (Dominant - Tonic). This is called *anticipation*.

Here is another classic - using major 7th and dominant 7th in one phrase. You see the note d, which belongs in the next bar, is played early, syncopated:

Here is a fast one, if you're playing a medium tempo song like Blue Moon, with triplets. Use open strings where possible to keep the fingering and bowing smooth. I have marked the position change to third position in the second bar:

Harmonically, Grappelli is delaying everything by half a bar. The *Em7* arpeggio is played on the *A7* chord, the *A7* arpeggio is played on the first half of the *D*. Sounds great!

A simpler version of the triplet lick is this, on a longer *II-V-I* cadence:

The next lick makes use of a phenomenon called 'alteration'. Let's have a look why that is the case.

Remember the Flat 9 Dominant lick on *A7* (*C#dim* is the name) in the Universal licks chapter, page 17? Well, this doesn't only work on a Minor key, but can be played over a Major cadence too, as a bit of colour.

When you play a Dominant lick made for a Minor key, on a Major key instead, you alter some notes from major to minor. Only do this on the Dominant chord. When you come back to the Tonic you use the major notes again.

In the following lick, Grappelli has altered two notes of the D major scale, in this case the 3rd and 6th notes (f# becomes f, b becomes b♭). This makes them minor. Try it out - it works great as long as you resolve to major (with an f# on *D* again).

You can do this Flat 9 alteration in any major key you like. Transpose this lick from D to G and C, and try out how it sounds.

To finish, here is an example of Grappelli's neat trick of playing three harmonics and an open string, in this case the A string. The first note is the open string, the second is a stretched fourth finger in third position, not pressed down. The third note is the second finger in third position, not pressed down, followed by the first finger, idem:

If you are not familiar with harmonics, check out the chapter about them in my first book "Stéphane Grappelli - Gypsy Jazz Violin" (*www.stephanegrappelli.com*). The notes should sound like this:

Track 43

Playalong solo on the chords of "Coquette" (D)

Listen to this playalong solo on Coquette. The form is the most common jazz form, AABA where 'B' stands for 'Bridge'. As before, I have used licks not only from the D major chapter but also from C and A major chapters, and when necessary transposed them. Find the original licks on the page numbers indicated.

Practise with your backing track!

Track 9

49

TIP #2: CHROMATIC NOTES

A great aspect of jazz is that we don't just use diatonic (scale) notes. The fun is in finding the more unexpected notes, to colour our phrases a bit differently: chromatic notes. These are scale notes that have been changed a semitone up (sharp) or down (flat). Let's look at the diatonic scale of C major first:

Now we throw in the chromatic notes as well (they're all the semitones between the diatonic notes), making it a chromatic scale:

Fingering is important. We don't want to lose our way in this scale with twelve different notes (the diatonic scale has only seven). The open strings of the violin should all be used. And the notes just below the open string should be played with the fourth finger. The first and second finger can slide. This gives us:

As you can see, the third finger only gets used once on the way - it doesn't slide like the first and second fingers. And the fourth finger only slides on the e string as there is no higher open string. Practise this fingering up and down (it's the same) and use it always. Here is a chromatic example from the Am chapter:

And here another, from the D major chapter:

LICKS IN F

F major is a key less often used by Grappelli - some old songs which he recorded in F with Django Reinhardt (like Honeysuckle Rose) he later started playing in D. But there are two standards he played in F all his life: How About You and Crazy Rhythm.

I've used the following recordings:

- Chicago (1937, Paris) - Quintette of the Hot Club of France
- Honeysuckle Rose (1938, London) - Quintette of the Hot Club of France
- Japanese Sandman (1939, Paris) - Quintette of the Hot Club of France
- How About You (1971, London) - Stéphane Grappelli Live
- Crazy Rhythm (1971, London) - Stéphane Grappelli
- Crazy Rhythm (1991, Tokyo) - Stéphane Grappelli Live

Tonic (*F*) licks

Sometimes, Grappelli played great licks with very simple notes. A simpler lick means it's easier to swing, and swing it does! Check out the following fragment from the song Chicago. The long upbeat takes place on the final turnaround of Django's solo, which means the lick really starts on the Dominant, *C7*, chord (the notes 'a' work on that very well because they are the 6th note of the *C7* chord).

When you play the second and third bars, don't rush the on-the-beat notes a, d and c. Play them late instead. Retaking the bow to play the d with a down bow helps.

Another simple lick, halfway into the solo, same timing on the upbeat but with some syncopation in the second bar:

In between the two is the following melody, with exactly the same beginning but starting on the fourth not third beat (remember the discussion on timing your lick on page 20?). The high f is played by sliding the fourth finger up very quickly, and sliding back again to a third position d:

Track 44

From the Quintette's recording of Japanese Sandman comes the following, much-used lick:

Honeysuckle Rose has longer Tonics and Dominants. Here is a long tonic example, with blue notes (e$^\flat$ and a$^\flat$) accented by some easy slides:

And here a long tonic lick from the 1971 recording of Crazy Rhythm - interesting bowing patterns, and check out the use of the note d, which suggests the chord *F6*:

From the same solo, a lick that uses the note b$^\flat$ (the 4th in F) as a bluesy kind of sound. Play this note long and with a bit of an accent to make it stick out.

With long licks like the three examples above, you can always take a little piece of the lick and use only that. Licks should be made to fit your own style and technique, so feel free to change them to whatever you need!

One of my favourite Grappelli licks in F is a lick that he used all his life. Here it is, taken from How About You:

Slide the third finger up to the high c, then stay in third position, playing both g and a with the first finger. The open A string is ghosted, which means you bow it, but only very lightly.

From How About You, this blues lick is a very good way of finishing a Tonic phrase. Don't use this all the time as it has a very distinctive sound, and you don't want people to hear you are repeating yourself too much:

And a more chromatic version, with the same notes but lots of non-blue notes in between, sounds like this (remember your chromatic fingering, using the open A string):

Track 45

As if to apologize for the blue notes a♭, e♭ and b♭, Grappelli throws in diatonic notes like the g, b and a and the result is very interesting: a mix of swing and blues.

Dominant (*C7*) licks

Here is a simple, old-fashioned lick on the Dominant, played by Grappelli during his solo on Honeysuckle Rose in 1938:

In bar 1, he plays the arpeggio of *B♭* (which has the same notes as *Gm7*, without the g). This is an example of playing Major on a Minor chord: the opposite of what I showed you in Tip #1 - Playing Minor on Major Chords (page 37).

On his recording of Japanese Sandman, Grappelli plays some classic lines. A 'model' lick is this dominant lick right at the start of his solo:

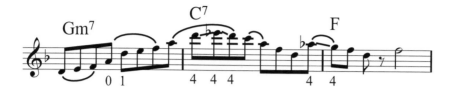

On page 61, check out Tip #3: Playing Minor on the Dominant. Here, Grappelli uses *Dm* notes on the Dominant cadence in F major: *Gm7 C7*. Even on the *F* chord, the tonic, he suggests *Dm* with the note d (which is the 6th in F).

Play the push-pull (slide up and down) and the pull (only down) in bar 2 with one finger, in this case the fourth. The bowing is old-fashioned, with many notes on one bow. You could change that if you like. And as always: when you change position to third, use the open A string.

The following lick is played on the long dominant progression (*Gm7 C7*) in How About You, right at the end of Grappelli's solo chorus (don't forget the correct chromatic fingering, try it here):

From the fast studio recording of Crazy Rhythm (1971) comes the following lick. See the irregular bowing pattern and the use of flat 5th (d♭) and flat 6th (e♭) notes on *Gm7* - giving it a really bluesy sound:

On the turnaround in F, which means you start on the Tonic but go to the Dominant by playing *I-VI-II-V*, Grappelli plays this triplet lick - a trick we saw in D major before:

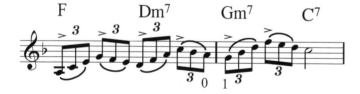

On the last note of bar 1, the open A string, change to third position and continue with the first finger on the g.

Here is an eighth note version of the same arpeggio licks, timed differently and simpler, on the turnaround of Crazy Rhythm, Live in Tokyo towards the end of Grappelli's life:

And another eighth note arpeggio lick on the 1971 studio version of Crazy Rhythm, with an interesting alteration: he turns the *Gm7* into a dominant, *G7*, with a flat 9th note (a♭):

Track 46

The *II* in *II-V-I* in a major key is always minor. In F major, the *II* is *Gm7*. In your solo, you can decide to alter this minor chord (well, you alter the notes *you* play, while the original chord gets played by the rhythm section) into a dominant chord (*G7*). The big change is of course the note b♭, which becomes b.

What you then do is make the *II* sound like a Dominant *II*, even if the rhythm section is still playing it minor. It gives more direction to your line, because the extra dominant wants to resolve, pushing the line forward.

We saw before that the flat 9th note is a welcome addition to any dominant chord. In this case, the flat 9th is a♭ and it adds a nice flavour to the altered sound.

Playalong solo on the chords of "Honeysuckle Rose" (F)

This Fats Waller song is useful not just in gypsy jazz jam sessions, but also in standard jazz sessions of all kinds. It is one of the most used jazz songs of all time. The form is AABA, 32 bars. Most licks in the following solo have been taken from various chapters, not just the one in F. Corresponding page numbers are annotated over each lick.

Track 10

Work with **Track 11** to practise your licks.

Track 11

56

LICKS IN D minor

Now we come to the less often-used keys. D minor is the key of one very well-known gypsy jazz song: I've Found A New Baby.

There are many great licks in D minor. The ones in this chapter come from two recordings of I've Found A New Baby, old and more recent:

- I've Found A New Baby (1937, Paris) - Django Reinhardt & Stéphane Grappelli
- I've Found A New Baby (1972, London) - Barney Kessel & Stéphane Grappelli

Tonic (*Dm*) licks

Let's start with the old version with Django. Recorded in duo, Grappelli doesn't even properly state the whole theme but starts improvising more or less straightaway, and does so all the way up to the (not very well rehearsed) end.

The song I've Found A New Baby starts in D minor but finishes in F major, just as It Don't Mean A Thing starts in G minor and finishes in B♭ major. Both these songs are a reminder of the relative minor and major we talked about earlier in Tip #1 (page 37). D minor is the relative minor of F major. They both have the same basic scale. So you can use a lot of licks from the previous chapter (F major)!

Grappelli's take on this song in the thirties has him playing mostly a b♭ (minor 6th) on D minor. He also plays the c♯ a lot, which makes it a harmonic scale:

Here is a first lick, using that scale, with a cool upbeat (I like the jump from the open A string to high b♭, and the long upbeat):

Another option is to play the major 6th, the note b, instead. From the seventies version with the great Barney Kessel, one of Grappelli's best albums ever, comes the following lick:

Focusing on the major 7th note, c#, Grappelli plays the following lick, which he uses from the seventies onwards on every minor tune (sometimes transposed, of course):

On minor keys, too, Grappelli loves the blue notes. Here is a common example with a flat 5th, which can be repeated a number of times if you want:

Now for a typical third position lick, from the older version of I've Found A New Baby, where you change back to first position using the open A string in the second bar:

A more riffy, rhythmical variant is this one - this can be repeated a number of times as it's nice and short:

Track 47

Thinking back to what I said about transposing licks, why not try a typical A minor shape on D minor? It just means bringing it down one string. Go back to page 38. Take the 2nd and 3rd lick and transpose them one string down - so in D minor they look like this:

and this:

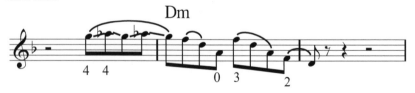

Dominant (*A7*) licks

The notes b♭ and c♯ from the harmonic scale, are used on the Dominant chord a lot. The c♯ is the 3rd and the b♭ is the flat 9th. On the thirties recording with Django, Grappelli plays:

The same notes are used on this dominant lick, a few bars later:

On the later recording, Grappelli plays a similar line with b♭ and c♯:

... and also a more melodic one:

A final, riffy, lick uses just the 'a's in octaves - this is the simplest of licks but very useful if you don't know anything more interesting to play, and very easy to transpose to other keys!

Track 48

59

Playalong solo on the chords of "I've Found A New Baby" (Dm)

This song, as discussed above, is really in two keys: Each A section starts in Dm and ends in F. So I've taken licks from both the D minor and F chapters for this solo. The form is AABA again, with a bridge. The second bar of all A sections suggests *A7*, but is normally accompanied with a *Dm* walking chord sequence, so you can play *Dm* licks on there.

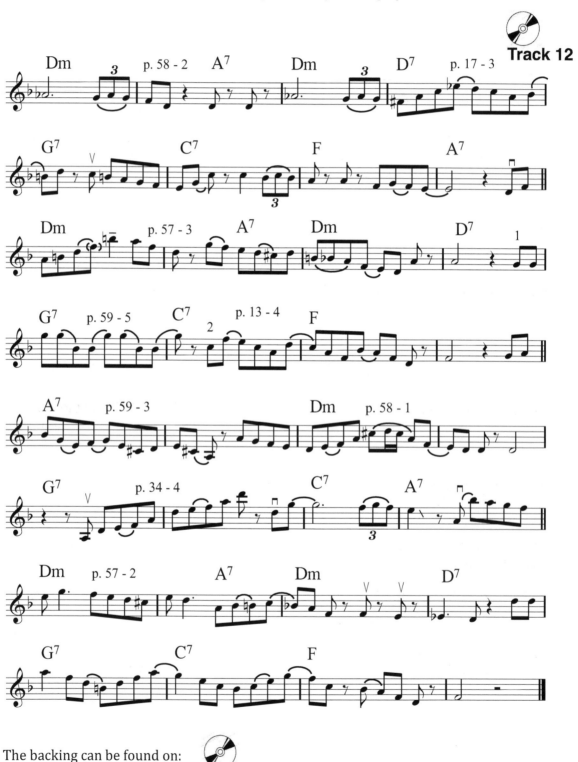

The backing can be found on:

Track 13

TIP #3: PLAYING MINOR ON THE DOMINANT

As we've seen before, one of the great things about jazz is that you can use your licks not only on chords that they were made for, but on some other chords as well.

This tip shows you how to play a Minor lick on a Dominant chord. In G major, whose dominant is *D7*, let's look at the *II* (*Am*) and the *V* (*D7*, with an added 9th).

You see, *Am* is part of *D7*! So we can play an *Am* lick on the *D7* chord, as both chords have the same scale (they are diatonic chords, *II* and *V*, in G major):

You can either play only diatonic notes, including a 'g' (the g is the minor 7th on the *Am* arpeggio) - then it sounds better if you come back to *D7* with an f♯ at the end:

Or, you can be a bit more adventurous and play a g♯ (this is the major 7th on the *Am* arpeggio, a great sound on *D7* called sharp 11th) - keeping the *Am* notes all the way:

So now you can play two things on the Dominant: its dominant (*V*) licks, or minor licks from its *II*. On *D7*, that is *Am*. On *G7*, that is *Dm*. And so on.

To finish, here is a Grappelli lick on *A7*, from the song It Had To Be You. His notes are based on the E minor arpeggio, which even has a flat 5th (b♭):

LICKS IN B♭

B♭ is a very useful one to know if you are playing with wind players: saxophones, clarinet or trumpet. Not the easiest of keys for the violin, it nevertheless has some great material. The open A and E strings can be used as chromatic notes and that sounds really good.

These are the three recordings that I have used in this chapter (all from the early years, as Grappelli didn't play much in B♭ later in his life):

- The Sheik Of Araby (1937, Paris) - Quintette of the Hot Club of France
- Charleston (1937, Paris) - Quintette of the Hot Club of France
- Fascinating Rhythm (1956, Paris) - Stéphane Grappelli

Tonic (*B♭*) licks

Let's start with The Sheik Of Araby. On this tune, Grappelli bases his whole solo around arpeggios. This is a good example, where he plays one arpeggio with the 6th (g) and major 7th (a) notes:

Another arpeggio line in the next chorus, using the same notes, but adding the sharp 5th (the note e) as a colour:

Here is a lick starting on the 9th (the note c), taken from the solo on Charleston. This lick was featured on page 53 already on a *Gm7* chord, but now it's played on *B♭*:

Repeating notes makes things easier for the left hand, and it still sounds interesting:

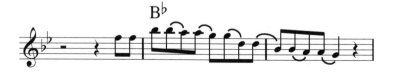

Using the leading notes to the arpeggio of $B^\flat$, Grappelli plays lines like this:

Here is what he does with this concept on Fascinating Rhythm, a very fast triplet version - see if you can do this:

Talking about very fast - this tonic lick starts off with an interesting sixteenth run, followed by a full chromatic octave (remember the fingering from Tip #2: Chromatic Notes, page 50?) On the track, I play it at 3 speeds:

Track 49

Dominant (*F7*) licks

We talked about playing Minor on the Dominant in Tip #3 (page 61). Here is a great example from the young Grappelli, on The Sheik Of Araby:

These are the arpeggio notes of C minor. *Cm* is related to *F7*, as we saw in Tip #3, because they have as common notes the c and e$^\flat$ (and arguably the g too). Try and transpose this 'alteration' to other dominant chords in this book.

Another, more altered lick, towards the end of the song - using the open E string as a leading note and with a raised 4th, b, in the first bar:

Track 50

A simple rhythmic approach always works. Double stops are a great sound and you can really swing them (as long as you stay with the beat - remember, straight eights!):

On Charleston, Grappelli plays the following dominant lick on the *II-V-I* in the theme. As you can see from the *C7* chord, this cadence has a dominant *II*, not a minor *II*. This is a common progression with the older, 1920s, songs:

The A string harmonic in bar 2 is played by sliding the fourth finger up to a stretched position, then coming back to third position for the following note g. From then on, stay in third position to the end.

On Fascinating Rhythm, there are many *II-Vs* so lots of chances to develop a nice line. Grappelli was listening to bebop in the fifties and it shows in his playing, although he is still using bits of the old thirties licks above:

Here is another one, with a flat 9th (g) and sharp 9th (a). Also very boppy!

Here is a final great lick on the dominant - starting with flat 9th and finishing on 'slow' quarter note triplets at the end:

Track 51

64

Playalong solo on the chords of "The Sheik Of Araby" (B♭)

Given the rather limited number of licks in B♭, and the number of non-diatonic chords in this song, I have gone all through the book selecting appropriate licks, transposing them or using them in a slightly different way on this solo. See if you can understand how I use the licks and why they work here.

Track 14

The backing can be found on:

Track 15

LICKS IN G minor

Like D minor, G minor is a rarely used key but it's worth looking at, as it's the key for Duke Ellington's classic, It Don't Mean A Thing If It Ain't Got That Swing and also Django's famous song, Minor Blues.

I have used the following recordings:

- Minor Blues (1949, Rome) - Quintette of the Hot Club of France
- It Don't Mean A Thing If It Ain't Got That Swing (1971, London) - Stéphane Grappelli

Tonic (*Gm*) licks

Let's start with Minor Blues - recorded in Rome in 1949, one of Django and Stéphane's last times together. Typically, Grappelli plays minor arpeggios on the Tonic, with a few extra notes added to them. Here is a third position lick - watch the open strings:

Grappelli often uses the 'call' which is a trumpet-like long note at the start of a phrase, like Louis Armstrong used to play. The following lick has a long call, starting on the second beat of the previous bar:

The Blues is a natural place for riffs, because the harmonies don't change very often. Here is a G minor riff, with a simple double stop, played short. The open A and E strings are ghosted - play the note very lightly, so that it's hardly heard:

On It Don't Mean A Thing Grappelli plays a similar riff, but bluesier, not with short but long notes. The raised 4th (c#) in the third bar is a sound he likes and uses a lot. Slide the third finger up on A and E strings, putting pressure on the bow for a bluesy sound.

Here's a lick that sounds as if it was inspired by Brahms' Hungarian Dance No. 5, but with a jazz lilt to it. The major 7th (f#) and major 6th (e) are part of the more modern Grappelli sound:

More of that sound on the Tonic chord in the beginning of the song. Use the chromatic fingering (page 50) on this lick:

Track 52

Dominant (D7♭9) licks

As we saw before, on a minor Tonic (Gm) the Dominant (D7) has a flat 9th. In this case, an e♭. Here is a lovely line that Grappelli plays in his solo on Minor Blues:

Another great line, using all the chromatic notes (especially the major 9th on D7, the note e, is an interesting one):

Track 53

67

On the statement of the melody of It Don't Mean A Thing, at the end of the bridge, Grappelli plays the following Dominant lick - delaying the *D7* dominant sound by not playing the f♯ too early - a great trick:

The same applies to a dominant bar early on in the solo - it's on *D7*, the *V*, but Grappelli plays the *Am7♭5* arpeggio: a, c, e, g, the *II*, on the first half of the bar, then the *D7♭9* on the second half of the bar (f♯, a, c, e♭). Remember, this is called playing Minor on the Dominant (Tip #3, page 61). It creates more tension by delaying the sound of the dominant until the second half of the bar:

Playalong solo on the chords of "Minor Blues" (Gm)

Minor Blues has 12 bars, like any other blues. I have played you two choruses of licks. Most of the licks are directly from the G minor chapter, as they are all classics. Note the *G7* chord in bar 4 and the *D7* chords in bars 9, 10 and 12 all resolve to minor, so I have used licks with the flat 9th (a$\flat$ on *G7* and e$\flat$ on *D7*).

Track 16

The backing track can be found on:

Track 17

TIP #4: BLUE NOTES

In Tip #2 (page 50), we looked at chromatic notes. These are diatonic or scale notes which have been made sharp or flat. Blue notes are chromatic notes too, but they're only ones that have been made flat.

In a major key, the most obvious blue note is the flat 3rd. This clashes with the major 3rd in the chord and that's exactly what we want. Try this out:

In a minor key, by the way, this is not a blue note - it's part of the scale (Cm has an e$^{\flat}$).

The next blue note is the flat 5th. In combination with the flat 3rd, this gives things a diminished sound. A bluesy clash with the natural 5th on the chord, in major or minor:

And finally, the major 7th becomes minor 7th, a sound we all know from blues singers or jazz composers like George Gershwin (Rhapsody in Blue):

Grappelli uses all these blue notes on his solos, as you will see. Sometimes only one of them, sometimes all of them. A question of taste!

To finish, here is the Blues Pentatonic scale: a great sound to play at the end of a solo. It finishes the phrase off completely. Pentatonic means five notes, and these include all the blue notes discussed above. Here is what is looks like, in C:

This is the most common version, but you can play these five notes: c, e$^{\flat}$, f, g$^{\flat}$ and b$^{\flat}$, in any order you like to make your own Blues Pentatonic lick.

LICKS IN A

The key of A major is never really used in jazz. Even in gypsy jazz, you will only really come across it on the song Django's Tiger, which was Django's simplified version of Tiger Rag, the Nick La Rocca hit in B♭.

Still, if you play with gypsy jazz guitarists, the chances are they'll want to play this song sooner or later, so we'd better prepare some licks in A! This is the famous recording you should listen to:

- Django's Tiger (1937, Paris) - Quintette of the Hot Club of France

Tonic (*A*) licks

Grappelli plays a classic solo. It's pretty much perfect in phrasing and the use of notes. Go and listen to it yourself. I could talk about every lick he plays, but only have space to select a few here for discussion.

The first lick is the start of Stéphane's solo. Nice and syncopated, with a long upbeat. Play upbows on the first two notes, it works:

And he continues with the same rhythmic pattern starting the next phrase on the Tonic - remember to always use open strings where possible, and on the chord of *A* that's quite often:

Track 54

Here are some blue notes - the minor 7th and flat 3rd, remember this from Tip #4 on page 70? The notes g and c.

Dominant (*E7*) licks

We've looked at Flat 9 Dominant chords and licks. On a major Tonic, you can choose to play a flat 9 dominant, as a special colour (in this key, the flat 9th is an f). Grappelli does this on Django's Tiger all the time. Here is the first example, early in his solo:

Another colour is to play the sharp 9th, g instead of g#, and combine this with the flat 9th. Then you get something like this:

Notice that Grappelli starts all these licks, tonic and dominant, on the second eighth note of the bar. This gives a feeling of speed, of rushing ahead. Here is a different start, with an upbeat:

Track 55

The notes in this lick are altered too. If you look at the arpeggio, it is that of *Bm7♭5*. There are two things going on here. First of all, the notes f suggest an altered Dominant, *E7♭9*, using the Flat 9th Dominant lick as described on page 17. But also, the *V* (*E7♭9*) is replaced by its *II* (*Bm7♭5*) as described Tip #3: Playing Minor on the Dominant, page 61.

This double alteration of the original *E7* chord is something that might seem terribly complicated, but Grappelli wouldn't have been thinking this way at all. In fact, I doubt if he was aware of the theory! Instead, using his ears, he chose to play one of the licks that he knew and that sounded cool on this particular chord. You should think the same way.

Playalong solo on the chords of "Django's Tiger" (A)

One of the classic Grappelli solos is his improvisation on Django's Tiger. I have added a few more licks from that recording which are not in the book, in the playalong solo, plus the usual transposed licks.

To practise your own licks, play the backing on:

Track 19

73

BUILDING YOUR SOLOS

Of course, you could take all the licks from this book, transpose them where necessary, and use them to fill your solos on all the gypsy jazz songs. The problem with that is, that you would sound like a computer talking Stéphane Grappelli-language.

What you want to do, is use the licks sparingly when you really need them, and for the rest make your own phrases and lines. You should be shaping the musical line of the solo yourself: how it starts, how it stops, where it is loud and soft. For that, you can only use your own musicality. But there are some licks to help you start, finish and take over a solo.

Breaks

It is a jazz tradition on the faster songs, to play a break on the Tonic chord at the end of the melody chorus before going into the solos. This is usually two bars long. With a *break*, I mean that the rhythm section drops out, creating a gap for the soloist.

It is one of the hardest things to play over a break. There is no support from the band. Your tempo has to be perfect and the notes clear enough for the band to come in together correctly at the start of the next chorus.

That is why it's a good idea to practice the phrases you use on a break. They are Tonic licks. Here are some Grappelli examples on the recordings used in this book.

The first break, in G major, is from Limehouse Blues (1972, London) - Barney Kessel & Stéphane Grappelli. It is played on the last 2 bars of the first chorus of the song, and the double barline indicates where the next chorus starts:

As you can see, a simple G major lick, with a bluesy flat 5th. Now a C major break on Swing 42 (1982, Saratoga, CA) - Stéphane Grappelli Live:

The band play a stop chord on the first beat. See how this one starts just *after* that, whereas the G major break above, started *before* the stop chord? The notes are very chromatic but the main sound is bluesy again (flat 3rd, minor 7th).

In D, there is a nice break on Grappelli's live Blue Moon (1990, Australia):

Here, Grappelli follows the implied harmony (the theme finishes on D major, followed by a quick dominant *A7* chord to go back to the top) - so on the second bar, he plays an *A7* dominant arpeggio.

From the live performance of Crazy Rhythm (1991, Tokyo) comes the following break:

Again, very bluesy through the flat 3rd and minor 7th. The break starts with an upbeat before the final F major Tonic, as you can see. The good thing about an upbeat is that it connects the rhythm all the way through.

There are a few things to be said about these breaks. First of all, syncopation is risky. If the band don't understand what you're doing, or if you're doing it less than perfect, they have a problem coming in together on the next chorus. So it's continuous eighth note patterns that work best.

Then the bluesy sound - I told you before that Grappelli often uses the blue notes at the end of a phrase. It's no different here: this is the end of the theme.

And finally, it's important that you continue your break all the way through to the downbeat of the first bar of the next chorus (where the double barline is). This, too, makes it very clear where you are, so you don't confuse the rhythm section. Don't stop early! Practise these breaks with a metronome.

Pickups

If you are not the first soloist, then somebody else will have improvised before you. You can only hope they make a nice ending to their solo (listen to Django and Stéphane, usually the first soloist gets softer and lower at the end to give the second soloist a chance to start).

Leaving a gap in the music is to be avoided. You want to keep the music going. Take over as soon as you can, while your colleague finishes his or her line. That's where the *pickup* comes in.

A pickup is a long upbeat that takes place on the last bar or bars of the previous soloist's solo. There will be a bar or so where one musician is finishing and the next is starting up, but that is what you want - it's like passing the baton in a relay race - don't drop it!

Here is a good example of a pickup on Minor Swing (1937, Paris) - Quintette of the Hot Club of France. The first solo is played by Django Reinhardt, and Grappelli takes over as follows, in the last bar of Django's final solo chorus. The double barline is where the next chorus starts:

On the recording of Charleston (1937, Paris) - Quintette of the Hot Club of France, Grappelli takes a one bar pickup again at the end of Django's solo. Notice it's the same timing, starting on the second eighth note of the bar:

Track 59

On the live performance of Crazy Rhythm (1991, Tokyo) he plays a much longer pickup, which contrasts nicely with the chord solo ending of his guitarist, Marc Fosset:

Looking at this long lick, I think it could also work as a Break: compare it with the example of Crazy Rhythm on the previous page.

The following pickup is on the live Swing 42 recording (1982, Saratoga, CA). Stéphane comes in during the last few chords of guitarist Martin Taylor's solo, again with a long, two-bar lick:

Track 60

As you can see, pickups have a kind of up-beat function, they introduce your solo before it really starts. Practice these licks and see if you can make your own upbeats, following the examples in this book.

Starting a song

In the old days with the Quintette, Django usually started the songs. He would often do this with a four bar chord intro. Later on, in the seventies, Grappelli was the main artist with his own band, and we hear him starting up songs himself, with some great single line licks.

The main thing is to be rhythmically absolutely perfect. You are setting the tempo and don't want any problems once the band join in. A starting lick replaces the count-in (which is where you say: "one, two, one two three four") so it should be just as clear.

The following eight bar lick is a great example of how Grappelli starts the song Sweet Georgia Brown (key of F major, but the first chord is *D7*). I took this from his 1972 recording, live in London:

After the double barline, the song starts with the melody. Meanwhile, the tempo has been set very clearly and everybody is feeling the beat before they start.

Here is an introduction to the song It Had To Be You, from Grappelli's live concert at the Grand Opera House (1986, Belfast):

Bar 4 shows you the upbeat for the melody of the song. Until then it's just continuous eight notes, to establish the beat.

Here is a more 'arranged' intro, which is performed together with guitarist Martin Taylor on the song Blue Moon (1990, Australia), live:

Track 61

Again, continuous eighth notes followed by the upbeat to the song. Let there be no mistaking where the bar lines are!

You can make your own intros for songs. The simpler the better - as long as they are in the right key and rhythmically strong.

Ending a song

When people come to listen to a concert, the things they will remember best are the beginning and the end. So it's very important that you know what to do when you finish your songs!

When rehearsing a song with your band, make sure you spend enough time on the ending. It could be any arrangement you like, as long as it is strong. A big help is when you and your colleagues have chosen some licks they are going to use on the end. Then it all comes together nicely and people will applaud when you want them to.

Some of the endings below I have already used on the playalong solos. Check back to listen to them played 'live'. All these endings can be transposed of course!

We'll start by looking at the typical Quintette 1930s endings. Here is the classic one from Minor Swing (1937) - you can hear it on the last two bars of **Track 6**:

Track 6

This can be used on any key, minor or major - here for example on G major on the Quintette's Limehouse Blues (1935):

A nice one in B♭ is the Grappelli ending on Charleston (Paris, 1937) - if you want you can listen to this on the end of **Track 14**:

Track 14

In 1962, the recording of Minor Swing features a much 'cooler' ending - check out the bowed ghost note, the bluesy flat 5th and the long end note:

Track 62

78

On the later recordings of songs in G major, such as How High The Moon or Lady be Good, Grappelli often plays something like the following lick:

Here is a variant, just double the fingering on both strings:

Track 63

And finally, an old Django trick on the *I-V-I* which is great on the violin too, for songs like Minor Blues (If you want, you can check back to the end of **Track 16** to hear it):

Track 16

CONCLUSION

That wraps up what I can teach you in this book. I hope you have found what you were looking for, and possibly a few things that you weren't looking for as well. Feel free to get in touch on *info@timkliphuis.com* with questions, or if you want to organise a lesson.

The most important thing I learnt from writing this is, how well Stéphane Grappelli placed his licks in the bar. Using a different timing every time makes the same lick sound new and fresh.

As I've said before, don't use licks like a machine, throwing out one after the other. A good solo is always a mix of your own material and other players' licks. When you are using a lick from this book, you are linking your playing up with history: the influence of Joe Venuti, Louis Armstrong and Art Tatum on Grappelli's playing is known, but those players all had their heroes as well. You can trace the origins of every lick in this book back to the birth of jazz. Isn't that great?

Take your time to learn things and come back to it often - repeating what you've learnt makes it really sink in. And then ... go out and surprise others with your new licks!